MEDITATIONS ON
THE WAY OF THE CROSS

MEDITATIONS ON THE WAY OF THE CROSS

by
Mother Teresa of Calcutta
and
Brother Roger of Taizé

THE PILGRIM PRESS
NEW YORK

First published in German under the title *Kreuzweg* by
Verlag Herder Freiburg im Breisgau in 1985.
The English edition first published 1986 by A.R. Mowbray
& Co. Ltd., Saint Thomas House, Becket Street, Oxford,
OX1 1SJ, England.

A list of sources and acknowledgments appears on page 60.
The biblical texts are from those used in the Common
Prayer at Taizé. They are based on *The New American Bible*,
the *Revised Standard Version of the Bible*, *The Jerusalem Bible*,
and *The Holy Bible: New International Version*. Extracts from
Mother Teresa of Calcutta, *A Gift for God*, ed. Malcolm
Muggeridge, are reproduced by permission of Collins Pub-
lishers.

Library of Congress Cataloging-in-Publication Data

Teresa, Mother, 1910–
    Meditations on the way of the cross.

    Translation of: Kreuzwig.
    1. Jesus Christ—Passion—Meditations.   I. Roger,
frère, 1915–   . II. Title.
BT431.T4513   1987   232.9'63   86-9313
ISBN 0-8298-0585-0

The Pilgrim Press, 132 West 31 Street
New York, NY 10001

MEDITATIONS ON
THE WAY OF THE CROSS

Suffering in itself is nothing; but suffering shared with Christ's passion is a wonderful gift. The most beautiful gift of human beings is that they can share in the passion of Christ. Yes, a gift and a sign of his love; because this is how God proved divine love for the world—by giving Jesus to die for us.

Mother Teresa

To travel far and join the poorest, is that living dangerously? Yes, but that's not all there is to it. Giving one's body to be burned, sharing one's goods, committing one's energies in the struggle for justice, is that living dangerously? Expending all one's strength to take part in the birth of a new humanity, could that be it, living dangerously? Yes, but that's not all there is to it. These commitments may be undertaken without a burning love.

Who, then, lives dangerously? The one who goes with Jesus through death to resurrection and is willing, with him, to give up even life for love.

Brother Roger

1. Jesus Is Condemned to Death

He was insulted and did not retaliate with insults; when he suffered, he made no threats. Instead he entrusted himself to the One who judges justly. . . . Through his wounds we have been healed. (1 Peter 2:23–24; see Isaiah 53:5–7)

Without looking back, you want to follow Christ: be prepared, in a life of great simplicity, to struggle with a reconciled heart.

Wherever you happen to be, do not be afraid of the struggle for the oppressed, whether believers or not. The search for justice calls for a life of concrete solidarity with the very poorest; . . . words alone can become a drug.

Prepare yourself as well, cost what it may, for that struggle within yourself to remain faithful to Christ until death. This continuity of an entire lifetime will create in you an inner unity which will see you through everything.

Struggling with a reconciled heart means being able to stand firm in the midst of crippling tensions. Far from smothering your energies, this kind of struggle challenges you to summon all your vital forces.

Your intentions may be misrepresented. If you remain unforgiving, if you refuse to be reconciled, what reflection of Christ are you giving? Without a prayer for your opponent, what darkness within you! If you lose the ability to forgive, you have lost everything.

By yourself you cannot do much for others. Together, in community, animated by the breath of Christ's loving, a way forward opens up leading from dryness to a common creation. And when a community is a ferment of reconciliation in that communion which is the Church, then the impossible becomes possible.

You try to be leaven in the dough, you try to love the Church, and so often you come up against internal divisions which tear apart Christ's Body, the Church. The mark of those who seek reconciliation is

4

that, following Christ, they long to fulfill more than to destroy, to understand more than to exhort. At all times they remain within, until the very weaknesses of the Church are transfigured.

Far from lighting short-lived blazes, give your life to the end, and day after day it will turn into a creation with God.

Brother Roger

I find the work much easier and I can smile more sincerely when I think of each one of my suffering brothers and sisters. Jesus needs you to keep pouring into the lamp of our life the oil of your love and sacrifice. You are really reliving the passion of Christ. Bruised, divided, full of pain and wounds as you are, accept Jesus as he comes into your life. . . . Without him we could do nothing. And it is at the altar that we meet our suffering poor. And in him that we see that suffering can become a means to greater love and greater generosity.

Mother Teresa

2. Jesus Carries His Cross

His state was divine, yet he did not cling to his equality with God, but made himself nothing, taking the very nature of a slave, and became as human beings are. (Philippians 2:6–7)

You are the God of all human beings, and since the dawn of time, you have inscribed within each person a law of love. But few there are who realize that you have created us in your image, free to love.

God, the living God, in your striving to make yourself understood, you came to earth in Christ Jesus as one of the poor.

And this Jesus, rejected, tortured on a cross, dead and laid in a tomb, you raised to life again.

No one can understand the death of Jesus without knowing him first as the Risen Lord. Then, in a flash, we glimpse the mystery:

O Christ, you ask us the very same question you asked your disciples: "Who do you say I am?"

You are the One who is alive. Risen from the dead, you are in agony with all who are afflicted. Your Spirit lives in everyone who undergoes human suffering.

You call upon each of us to follow you. And following you means taking up our own cross every day. But you come down to where we are, down to the very depths, to take upon yourself all that weighs us down. You remain alongside each one of us. You even go and visit those who died before they could possibly know you (1 Peter 3:19–20).

The contemplation of your boundless mercy becomes a radiant goodness in the humble hearts that let themselves be led by your Spirit.

Brother Roger

God has identified with the hungry, the sick, the naked, the homeless; hunger, not only for bread, but for love, for care, to be somebody to someone; nakedness, not of clothing only, but nakedness of that compassion that very few people give to the unknown; homelessness, not only just for a shelter made of stone, but that homelessness that comes from having no one to call your own. . . .

Without our suffering, our work would just be social work, very good and helpful, but not the work of Jesus Christ, not part of the redemption. Jesus wanted to help by sharing our life, our loneliness, our agony, our death. Only by being one with us has he redeemed us.

We are asked to do the same; all the desolation of the poor people, not only their material poverty, but their spiritual destitution, must be redeemed. And we must share it, for only by being one with them can we redeem them by bringing God into their lives and bringing them to God.

Mother Teresa

3. Jesus Falls for the First Time Under the Weight of the Cross

Like one from whom we hide our faces, he was despised and we took no account of him. *(Isaiah 53:3)*

A boy talks to me about an inner drama.

His suffering goes on and on. There is nothing more cruel than a love rejected or broken off. The heart does not know how to react and, sometimes, as a way of defending itself against too much suffering, it grows hard. And then an antidote arises: self-love. From humiliation that is not accepted, the pride of life and human ambition are born.

When Christ is rejected, he does not rebel. He suffers and he loves.

A youth asks: How can a reconciliation come about when the other refuses?

That refusal is like a little death which makes us lose our footing. It is not easy for us to pick ourselves up again. Nothing hurts so deeply as to find someone with whom we are seeking reconciliation cold and distant. Our heart is wounded to the very depths.

It can even happen that forgiveness leads the other to this cynical calculation: why not go on farther with my plan, even to the point of trampling the other person underfoot, because in any case he or she will pardon me for Christ's sake?

If the other persists in refusal, does that mean that God does not answer prayer? Actually God has already answered "in ourselves." The answer was given "within us"; God has already reconciled us within.

I wrote to someone close to me, on the eve of an important day:

When the humiliated person in you would like to shake off everything he considers a dead weight, don't forget that this weight may be the easy yoke of Christ, his arm around your shoulders. When the stranglehold of rebellion makes you despair to the point of forsaking the Christ who called you once and for all, return to the inner oasis, the place of solitude within yourself; there, he repeats over and over again the same call. Of you he asks much—he has richly blessed you with gifts. Do not cast away these precious pearls by wasting your energies in finding out who was right and who was wrong. Let your life be a response of wonder at all he has placed within you.

Brother Roger

We picked up a young man from the streets of Calcutta. He was very highly educated and had many degrees. He had fallen into bad hands and had his passport stolen. After some time I asked him why he had left home. He said his father did not want him. "From childhood he never looked me in the eyes. He became jealous of me, so I left home." After much praying, the Sisters helped him to return home, to forgive his father, and this has helped both of them. This is a case of very great poverty.

Mother Teresa

4. Jesus Meets His Mother

Love is as strong as death.   (The Song of Songs 8:6)

We are both aware that vast regions of the world are covered by spiritual deserts. There you find young people marked by human abandonment and subtle doubt, the result of broken relationships which affect them to their very depths.

Even when they are thirsting for a spiritual life, many of the young are afflicted by doubt. They are unable to place their confidence in God, to believe, since they have not found confidence in those to whom life had entrusted them. Separations have wounded the innocence of their childhood or adolescence. The consequences are skepticism and discouragement: What's the use of living? Does life still have any meaning?

In Calcutta, there are visible homes for the dying. In Western civilization, many of the young are in homes for the dying that are invisible, but nonetheless real. There are parents who, although they take care of material needs, are in fact totally absent in the eyes of their children.

The separation of generations has still other consequences: old people are forced to end their life in isolation. Even though they have enough to live on materially, it is as if they had nothing else before them but to wait for death. And yet, persons advancing in age so often know how to listen to others with such comprehension.

And so, in this time of painful separations and upheavals, we venture to address together an appeal to people of all ages:

To be alive, and not half-dead, seek Jesus who is alive. Seek him even if you seem to have lost him. He loves you. Finding him, you will find everything: love, peace, trust. Then life is worth living.

We, all of us, can become creators of peace and reconciliation wherever we happen to be. May our homes, however modest they may be, become like the house of Mary in Nazareth: a place to listen to others and to remain alongside them, in order to enable them to find a way out of the present crisis of confidence.

Saint John, in his great age, could only keep repeating: God is love. Where God is, there is love. If you love one another, says Jesus, all will know that you are my disciples. Let us bring the love of Jesus to the lonely, the sad, the sick, the depressed. In this way, many others will pass from discouragement and doubt to confident trust in the Spirit of the living God. Young and not-so-young will become a ferment of the peace and reconciliation that are so essential today, not only among believers, but in the entire human family.

Mother Teresa and Brother Roger

5. Simon of Cyrene Helps Jesus to Carry His Cross

Carry each other's burdens, and in this way you will fulfill the law of Christ. *(Galatians 6:2)*

Choosing Christ! He confronts us with an alternative: "Whoever would save their life will lose it. Whoever give their life for love of me will find it." But Christ does not impose the choice. He leaves each one free to choose him or to reject him. He never forces us. Simple, gentle, and humble of heart, he has been standing for two thousand years at the door of every human heart and knocking: "Do you love me?"

When it seems that the ability to respond to him has disappeared, we can only call out: "Give me the gift to give myself, to rest in you, O Christ, in body and in spirit."

Choosing Christ means walking on one road only, not on two roads at the same time. Whoever want both to follow Christ and to follow themselves would be setting out to follow their own shadow, in pursuit of reputation or social prestige.

Brother Roger

What do you ask of us, O Christ? Above all to carry one another's burdens, and to entrust them to you in our prayer, which always remains poor.

You welcome all who come to you with their burdens, and it is as if, anytime, anywhere, you welcomed them into your house in Nazareth.

When we let ourselves be welcomed by you, the suffering Servant, the inward eye perceives, beyond our own confusion, a reflection of the Christ of glory, the Risen Lord.

And we are brought to life each time you visit us by the Holy Spirit, the Comforter.

Brother Roger

6. Veronica Wipes the Face of Jesus

Your face, Lord, I seek.
Do not hide your face from me.   (Psalm 27:8–9)

You are God.
You are God from God.
You are Begotten, not made.
You are One in Substance with the Father.
You are the Son of the Living God.
You are the Second Person of the Blessed Trinity.
You are One with the Father.
You are in the Father from the beginning;
    All things were made by You and the Father.
You are the Beloved Son,
    in whom the Father is well pleased.
You are the Son of Mary,
    conceived by the Holy Spirit in the womb of Mary.
You were born in Bethlehem.
You were wrapped in swaddling cloths by Mary
    and put in the manger full of straw.
You were kept warm by the breath of the donkey
    who carried your Mother with you in her womb.
You are the Son of Joseph,
    the carpenter as known by the people of Nazareth.
You are an ordinary man without much learning,
    as judged by the learned people of Israel.

Who is Jesus to me?

Jesus is the Word made Flesh.
Jesus is the Bread of Life.
Jesus is the Victim offered for our sins on the Cross.
Jesus is the Sacrifice offered at the Holy Mass for the
    sins of the world and mine.
Jesus is the Word   to be spoken.
Jesus is the Truth   to be told.
Jesus is the Light   to be lit.

Jesus is the Life   to be lived.
Jesus is the Love   to be loved.
Jesus is the Joy   to be shared.
Jesus is the Peace   to be given.
Jesus is the Bread of Life   to be eaten.
Jesus is the Hungry   to be fed.
Jesus is the Thirsty   to be satiated.
Jesus is the Naked   to be clothed.
Jesus is the Homeless   to be taken in.
Jesus is the Sick   to be healed.
Jesus is the Lonely   to be loved.
Jesus is the Unwanted   to be wanted.
Jesus is the Leper   to wash her wounds.
Jesus is the Beggar   to give him a smile.
Jesus is the Drunkard   to listen to him.
Jesus is the Mentally Ill   to protect him.
Jesus is the Little One   to embrace her.
Jesus is the Blind   to lead him.
Jesus is the Dumb   to speak to her.
Jesus is the Crippled   to walk with him.
Jesus is the Drug Addict   to befriend him.
Jesus is the Prostitute   to remove from danger
   and befriend her.
Jesus is the Prisoner   to be visited.
Jesus is the Old   to be served.

To me

Jesus is my God
Jesus is my Spouse
Jesus is my Life
Jesus is my only Love
Jesus is my All in All
Jesus is my Everything.

23

Jesus, I love with my whole heart, with my whole being. I have given him all, even my sins and he has espoused me to himself in tenderness and love. Now and for life I am the Spouse of my Crucified Spouse. Amen.

Mother Teresa

7. Jesus Falls the Second Time

My palate is drier than a potsherd and my tongue is stuck to my jaw. I am lying in the dust of death. (Psalm 22:15)

I am haunted by a sight I saw in Bangladesh. In a narrow alleyway, a child was crouched on the ground, carrying a baby on one arm, and trying with the other to lift a second baby. When he held them both, he collapsed. An image of the wounded innocence of childhood. Why is it not possible to take care of such children? More than a year afterward my heart has not recovered.

Brother Roger

In England and other places, in Calcutta, in Melbourne, in New York, we find lonely people who are known by the number of their room. Why are we not there? Do we really know that there are some people, maybe next door to us? Maybe there is a blind woman who would be happy if you would read the newspaper for her; maybe there is a rich person who has no one to visit him—he has plenty of other things, he is nearly drowned in them, but there is not that touch and he needs your touch. Some time back a very rich man came to our place, and he said to me: "Please, either you or somebody, come to my house. I am nearly half-blind and my wife is nearly mental; our children have all gone abroad, and we are dying of loneliness, we are longing for the loving sound of a human voice."

Mother Teresa

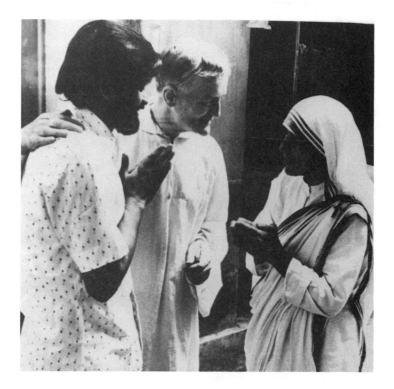

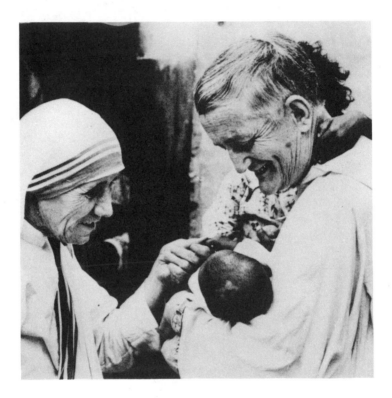

8. Jesus Consoles the Women of Jerusalem Who Weep for Him

They will look on the one whom they have pierced, and weep for him as for a first-born child. *(Zechariah 12:10)*

O God, the God of everybody, you ask us all to bring love where the poor are humiliated, joy where the Church is downcast, and reconciliation where people are divided—fathers and sons, mothers and daughters, husbands and wives, believers and those who cannot believe, Christians and their unwanted fellow Christians. You open this way for us, so that the broken body of Jesus Christ, your Church, may be leaven of communion for the poor of the earth and in the whole human family.

Brother Roger

We are both of us challenged by the sufferings of the modern world. Confronted with all that wounds humanity, we find the divisions between Christians unbearable.

Are we ready to set aside our separations, freeing ourselves from our fear of one another? When people differ, what use is there in trying to find who was right, who was wrong?

In our search for reconciliation, are we ready to learn ways of offering the best of ourselves, of welcoming what is best in others, loving one another in the way Jesus loves us?

We thank you, Christ Jesus, because the Catholic Church is the Church of the Eucharist, rooted in your words "This is my body, this is my blood," and so giving life by your adorable presence.

We thank you, because the Protestant Churches are the Churches of the Word, and constantly recall the power of your gospel.

We thank you, because the Orthodox Churches, so often in their history, are brought by faithfulness to go to the very extremes of loving.

So, Christ, give us all openness to ways leading beyond our own selves: may we no longer delay reconciliation in that unique communion called the Church, irreplaceable leaven set in the midst of humanity.

Mother Teresa and Brother Roger

9. Jesus Falls the Third Time

In my own body I make up what is still to be undergone by Christ for the sake of his body, which is the Church. (Colossians 1:24)

In Leningrad Cathedral, Bishop Nicodim asked me to speak to the young people:

If Christ were not risen, we would not be here. There would be nothing in the whole country of the burning confidence which is yours.

Just before that, I addressed those who would soon be priests:

The more you walk with Christ, the more you will be led on to the mountain of temptation. He himself was there. The closer we draw, invisibly, to the agony of Christ, the more we bear in ourselves a reflection of the Risen Lord.

Brother Roger

In a black neighborhood of Cape Town, where we thought we would be meeting just a few friends, a whole crowd had gathered for prayer. They were singing. Human voices can express the call from the depths more powerfully than anything else.

I tried then to express all that was in my heart by a gesture. I explained to the Africans: I would like to ask your forgiveness, not in the name of the whites, I could not do that, but because you are suffering for the gospel and you go before us into the kingdom of God. I would like to pass from one to another of you so that each of you can make the sign of the cross on my palm, the sign of Christ's forgiveness.

This gesture was understood immediately. Everyone made it, even the children. It seemed to take an eternity. Spontaneously they burst into songs of resurrection.

Brother Roger

A girl came from outside India to join the Missionaries of Charity. We have a rule that the very next day new arrivals must go to the Home for the Dying. So I told this girl: "You saw Father during Holy Mass, with what love and care he touched Jesus in the Host. Do the same when you go to the Home for the Dying, because it is the same Jesus you will find there in the broken bodies of our poor." And they went. After three hours the newcomer came back and said to me with a big smile—I have never seen a smile quite like that—"Mother, I have been touching the body of Christ for three hours." And I said to her: "How—what did you do?" She replied: "When we arrived there, they brought a man who had fallen into a drain, and been there for some time. He was covered with wounds and dirt and maggots, and I cleaned him and I knew I was touching the body of Christ."

Mother Teresa

10. Jesus Is Stripped of His Garments

There they are staring at me, glaring: they divide my garments among them and cast lots for my clothing. (Psalm 22:17–18)

In this age when the claims of human rights have come home to our consciences as never before, the law of "might is right" still rampages over the earth. Humanity is experiencing violence, rumors of war, armed conflicts.

In the gospel, peace bears the weighty name of reconciliation. This word requires commitment and can take us very far. Being reconciled means beginning a whole new relationship; it is a springtime of our being. What is true between individuals goes for nations too. What a springtime a reconciliation of nations would be, especially between East and West!

A whole young humanity on both hemispheres is eagerly waiting for the barriers that separate peoples to be brought down, and is not afraid to take risks for world peace. All these young people have certain basic characteristics:

In their search for peace, they refuse to uphold sacred egoisms, whether of a continent, a nation, a race, or a generation.

They are aware that, among the prerequisites for world peace, the most urgent is a fair distribution of the goods of the earth among all. The inequitable distribution of wealth, especially when held by Christians, is a wound inflicted upon the whole human community. Many ask: How is it possible that Christians, who often come to share spiritual goods, have in general, in the course of their history, managed so rarely to share their material goods?

Young seekers after peace also know that only equal trust shown to all the peoples of the earth, and not just to a few of them, can lead to the healing of the wounds that tear them apart. And so it is essential never to humiliate the members of a nation whose leaders have committed inhuman acts. Essential also is boundless concern for so many men and women who today, as exiles or immigrants, live on foreign soil. If every home were open to somebody of foreign origin, the racial problem would be partially solved.

In order to share material goods better between North and South, to repair breaches between East and West, sincerity of heart is necessary. Who, whether a political leader or not, could appeal for peace and not achieve it within him- or herself? "Be upright of heart and steadfast," wrote Sirach the Sage twenty-two centuries ago.

In the critical situations of our time, many are prepared to anticipate, in their lives, trust between nations. They seek in God the energies to persevere; they commit all their inner and spiritual resources to anticipate peace and reconciliation, not on the surface but in the depths. They know that they are not called to struggle with the weapons of power, but with a heart at peace. They refuse to take up partisan positions.

Peace begins in oneself. But how can we love those who oppress the weak and the poor? And harder still: how can we love our opponents when they profess faith in Christ? God moves us to pray even for those who hate. God is wounded with the innocent.

"Love your enemies, do good to those who hate you, pray for those who malign you." Making one's own these words of the Gospel requires maturity, and also the experience of having crossed inner deserts of our own.

In that ocean underlying human consciousness there is a longing. Day and night, it receives the answer: peace.

O Christ, sometimes we are strangers on this earth, disconcerted by all the violence, the harsh oppositions.

Like a gentle breeze, you breathe upon us the Spirit of peace.

Transfigure the deserts of our doubts and prepare us to be bearers of reconciliation wherever you place us, until a hope of peace arises in our world.

Brother Roger

11. Jesus Is Nailed to the Cross

Today you will be with me in paradise.   *(Luke 23:43)*

Jesus our joy. Jesus our life. He wants to bring each one of us to life. He gives himself, he heals. Through him, God offers us a serene joy, not unhappiness.

Throughout the world, the innocence of young people is very often wounded when their most sincere intentions are distorted, when their love is rejected. Recently, during a stay in Haiti in a miserable shantytown, a child who had nothing, not even a shred of clothing, insisted: "Take me with you (!)"; and the other children around him cried out: "Yes, he has no mother"—nor father. In that shantytown so many faces revealed each day a reflection of Christ on the Cross.

There are also human abandonments in the Northern Hemisphere but they are more hidden, less easily seen. Thus a very young boy from one city said about the parable of the prodigal son: "In my family, it's not I, the son, who have gone, it is my father who has left us."

Faced with human abandonments which cut off the young from the meaning of existence, from where can we draw the vital trust for life? The Risen Christ, who exists in the radiance of God, is at the same time in anguish, today, tomorrow, and until the end of the world. To understand Jesus' death on the cross it is necessary first of all to grasp that he is risen, and that at every moment he comes to meet us just as we are. He descends to the lowest point of our human condition. He takes upon himself all that hurts us, in ourselves and in others. He remains alongside those who are forced to undergo a kind of little death through the effects of contempt and the violence of hate.

Brother Roger

44

"I kept the Lord ever before my eyes because he is ever at my right hand that I may not slip."

The true inner life makes the active life burn forth and consume everything. It makes us find Jesus in the dark holes of the slums, in the most pitiful miseries of the poor, in the God-man naked on the cross, mournful, despised by all, the man of suffering, crushed like a worm by the scourging and the crucifixion.

What does our Society expect of its members? To be co-workers of Christ in the slums. Where will we fulfill that aim? Not in the houses of the rich, but in the slums. That is our kingdom. That is Christ's kingdom and ours, the field we have to work in. If a boy leaves his father's field and goes to work in another, he is no longer his father's co-worker. Those who share everything are partners giving love for love, suffering for suffering. Jesus, you have given everything, life, blood, all. Now it is our turn. We should put everything into the field also.

. . . Our prayers should be burning words coming forth from the furnace of a heart filled with love.

Mother Teresa

To be a true Christian means the true acceptance of Christ, and the becoming of another Christ one to another. To love as we are loved, and as Christ has loved us from the Cross, we have to love each other and give to others.

Mother Teresa

12. Jesus Dies on the Cross

My God, my God, why have you deserted me?   (Mark 15:34; see Psalm 22:1)

On the cross Jesus believes himself abandoned: "My God, my God, why have you forsaken me?" Seeing those who are torturing him, he prays: "Father, forgive them, for they do not know what they are doing." And from that day, for each one of us, the contemplation of his forgiveness gives rise to a radiance of goodness in the humble heart which lets itself be led by his Spirit.

We have eyes for looking, and our gaze needs to linger on the face of Jesus on the cross. Some artists have managed to communicate this face of Christ to an extent that enables us to enter into the mystery simply by looking. Among other things, we grasp that Christ Jesus leaves each person free to choose him, or to reject him. He never forces anyone. Simply, for nearly two thousand years, he stands at the door of every human heart and knocks: Do you love me? Will you remain with me to watch and pray for the people of the earth who are suffering from the abandonment of those they love, or suffering under hate and torture? Even without knowing how to pray we can all hold ourselves in the presence of the one who is risen. And in the long silences when it seems nothing is happening, we strengthen ourselves within, it is there that the best in us is built up.

Brother Roger

When Christ said, "I was hungry and you fed me," he didn't mean only the hunger for bread and for food; he also meant the hunger to be loved. Jesus himself experienced this loneliness. He came among his own and his own received him not, and it hurt him then and it has kept on hurting him. The same hunger, the same loneliness, the same having no one to be accepted by and to be loved and wanted by. Every human being in that case resembles Christ in his loneliness; and that is the hardest part, that's real hunger. . . .

If sometimes our poor people have had to die of starvation, it is not because God didn't care for them, but because you and I didn't give, were not instruments of love in the hands of God, to give them that bread, to give them that clothing; because we did not recognize him, when once more Christ came in distressing disguise—in the hungry woman, in the lonely man, in the homeless child, and seeking for shelter.

Mother Teresa

Death is going home, yet people are afraid of what will come so they do not want to die. If we do, if there is no mystery, we will not be afraid. There is also the question of conscience—"I could have done better." Very often as we live, so we die. Death is nothing but a continuation of life, the completion of life. . . . This life is not the end; people who believe it is, fear death. If it was properly explained that death was nothing but going home to God, then there would be no fear.

Mother Teresa

13. Jesus Is Taken Down from the Cross and Laid in the Arms of His Mother

I am the Lord's servant, may it be to me as you have said.   (Luke 1:38)

In Haiti we went several times to visit an old black woman who welcomes the poor and destitute in her house. One day this woman prayed, full of compassion: "I suffer because as soon as we have helped one human in distress, another person is already here with more suffering." To be truly alive means loving with a heartfelt compassion like that old woman, it means understanding others both in their joys and in their sufferings.

In the communion which is called the Church, the sacrament of reconciliation and the presence of Christ in the Eucharist are sources which open us to the compassion of God. We can thus make our own the ancient prayer: "Do not look on our sins, but on the faith of your Church."

Nowadays many people are searching for Christ and yet leave him abandoned when it comes to the unique communion of his Body, the Church. There, Christ is forsaken as rarely before.

Nevertheless, the more the Church is a land of compassion and reconciliation, the more it becomes both maternal in the likeness of Mary and called to joy: "Rejoice Mary, full of grace! Rejoice Church, full of grace! Rejoice my soul, full of grace!"

Also, to each person I would like to say: In order to be a leaven of the joy of Jesus, and to stay with him in his agony, will you prepare yourself, day by day, to trust in the faith of the Church? Clothed with compassion and with God's forgiveness, as with a garment, will you open up ways to reduce suffering across the earth? Wherever there are human abandonments, will you be a leaven of the trust which comes from the heart?

Brother Roger

O Christ, when you offer us life as reconciled people in the communion of your Body, your Church, you tear us out of our isolation and give us support in the faith of your whole Church, from the first Christians, the apostles and Mary, down to those of the present day.

We thank you for the reflection of your face, in those children who disclose your mysterious presence to us, exposing us to the realities of the kingdom—an overflowing heart, simplicity, wonder, and jubilation.

Brother Roger

Our Lord himself has promised a reward even for a cup of water given in his name. It is for his sake that we become beggars.

In fact he often endured real want, as the stories of the multiplication of the loaves and fishes and the plucking of the ears of corn on walks through the fields teach us. The thought of these instances should be salutary reminders whenever in the mission or at home our meals are meager. . . . Our Lord on the cross possessed nothing. . . . He was on the cross that was given by Pilate. The nails and the crown were given by the soldiers. He was naked and, when he died, cross, nails, and crown were taken away from him. He was wrapped in a shroud given by a kind heart, and buried in a tomb that was not his. Yet Jesus could have died as a king, and he could have risen from the dead as king. He chose poverty because he knew in his infinite knowledge and wisdom that it is the real means of possessing God, of conquering God's heart, of bringing God's love down to this earth.

"Whatsoever you do to the least of my brethren, you do it to me. This is my commandment that you love one another." Suppress this commandment and the whole grand work of the Church of Christ falls in ruins. . . .

Charity for the poor must be a burning flame in our Society. And just as when a fire ceases to burn, it is no longer useful and gives no more heat, so the day our Society loses its charity toward the poor, it will lose its usefulness and there will be no life.

Charity for the poor is like a living flame. The drier the fuel, the brighter it burns; that is, when our hearts are separated from earthly motives and completely united to the will of God, we shall be able to give free service. . . . The more united we are to God, the greater will be our love and readiness to serve the poor wholeheartedly. The more repugnant the work or the person, the greater also must be a Sister's faith, love, and cheerful devotion in ministering to our Lord in this distressing disguise.

Mother Teresa

14. Jesus Is Placed in the Tomb

If we become united with Christ through a death like his, we will certainly be united with him in his resurrection. (Romans 6:5)

Lord, help us to see in your crucifixion and resurrection an example of how to endure and seemingly to die in the agony and conflict of daily life, so that we may live more fully and creatively. You accepted patiently and humbly the rebuffs of human life, as well as the tortures of your crucifixion and passion. Help us to accept the pains and conflicts that come to us each day as opportunities to grow as people and become more like you. Enable us to go through them patiently and bravely, trusting that you will support us; for it is only by dying with you that we can rise with you.

Mother Teresa

The temptation of doubt puts our trust in God to the test. It can purify as gold is purified by fire. It can also cast a human being down into the bottom of a well. But there is still always a light shining from above. The darkness is never total. It never invades the whole person completely. God is present even in that darkness.

Harrowed by the trial of doubt, all who want to live the gospel allow themselves to be reborn day after day by the confidence of God. And life finds meaning again.

The meaning of life cannot be drawn from the clouds or from opinions; it is nourished by a trusting. God sends this trust like a breath of the Spirit falling upon every human being.

One of the irreplaceable marks of the gospel is that God invites human beings to place their confidence in turn in One who has come out of the grave and is alive. Faith is not an opinion, it is an attitude: the believer welcomes the Risen Lord and so becomes alive, not half-dead. Already in the early days of the Church, Irenaeus of Lyons, a Christian of the third generation after Christ—he had known Polycarp who had himself been a disciple of John the Evangelist—wrote: "The glory of God is a human being fully alive. The life of a human being is the vision of God."

O Christ, the meaning of our lives lies in your confidence in us. We tell you: "Lord, I believe, come and help my lack of trust." And you open for us a way of creation. Along this way, you show us how to create even with our own weaknesses.

Praise to the Risen Christ who, knowing how poor and vulnerable we are, comes and prays in us the hymn of an unchanging confidence.

Brother Roger

Sources

Brother Roger, *The Wonder of a Love* (Mowbray)
Brother Roger, *And Your Deserts Shall Flower* (Mowbray)
"Letter from Taizé" (bimonthly)
Jubilaeum Juvenum, pontificium concilium pro laicis, Vatican 1984
Mother Teresa of Calcutta, *A Gift for God,* ed. Malcolm Muggeridge (Wm. Collins Ltd, London, 1975)
Mother Teresa of Calcutta, *The Love of Christ* (Fount Paperbacks, 1982)